Designed by Flowerpot Press
www.FlowerpotPress.com
CHC-0909-0609
ISBN: 978-1-4867-2981-4
Made in China/Fabriqué en Chine

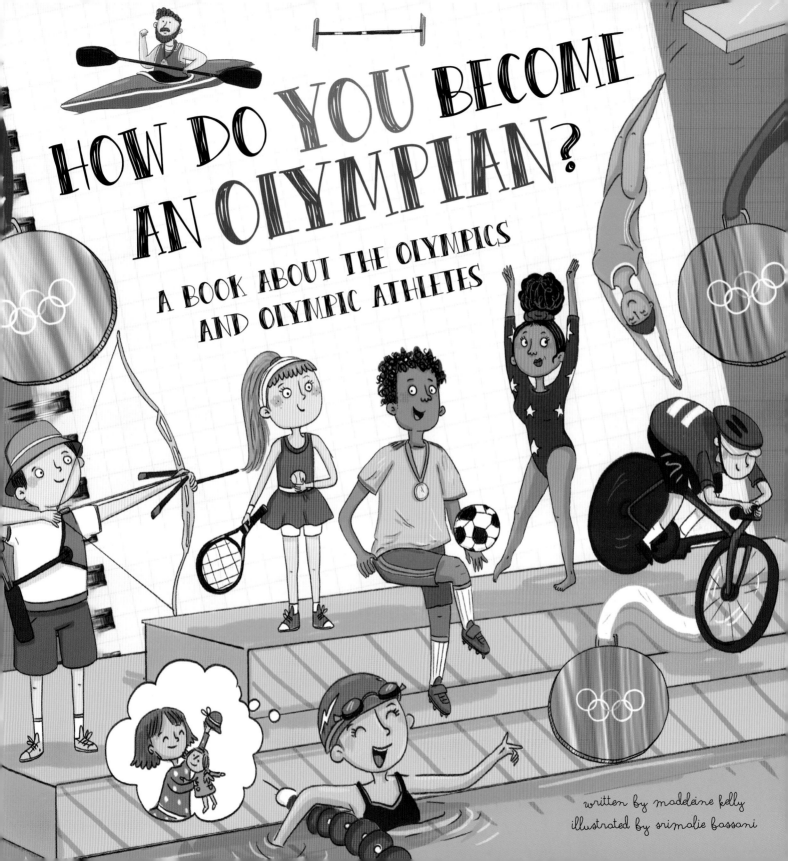

HOW DO YOU BECOME AN OLYMPIAN?

A BOOK ABOUT THE OLYMPICS AND OLYMPIC ATHLETES

written by maddeine kelly

illustrated by srimalie bassani

How do Olympians run so fast? Jump so high? Throw so far? Olympians are a group of people who are dedicated, tough, and hardworking, which is how they became the best in their event.

We get to watch them compete on TV every two years and are inspired to be dedicated, tough, and hardworking just like them. But what makes Olympians extra cool is that they're people who aren't very different from us. Before they were Olympians, they were kids playing music, playing tag, and playing dress up—just like you!

How did the Olympics come to be? Have the Olympics existed since before the dinosaurs?

The Olympics aren't quite that old! The first ever Games were held in 776 B.C. They began as an antidote to war. The Games encouraged athletes to put down their weapons and compete against each other in a nonviolent pursuit. Competitors from different Greek city-states would compete against each other so their citizens could cheer on their home team. It was designed as a way to bring people together.

GREECE

OLYMPIA

FUN FACT
In the early Olympics athletes competed naked!

The ancient Games took place in Olympia. Back then only Greek men were allowed to compete. Some of the events consisted of wrestling, sprinting, chariot racing, and even a type of fighting!

The Olympics were eventually banned by the Romans and wouldn't be brought back for over 1,500 years!

The first modern Games took place in 1896 in Greece and included more than 200 athletes from 14 countries. Now the Olympics includes about 11,000 athletes from 186 countries! Olympians come from all over the world. Athletes can come from small towns, big cities, and every continent. The Games are also held around the world. Instead of only taking place in Greece, 19 different countries have hosted the Olympics.

You're going to be an Olympian, kid!

How do you become an Olympic athlete? Are Olympians born knowing they'll become an athlete one day?

Olympians aren't born athletes—they become athletes! School is the place that many Olympians are introduced to sports. When they have a lot of fun playing a particular game, they join a team or other athletes who play the same sport. They go to competitions with their friends, they win together, and sometimes, they lose together.

Are you sure about this?

If a person excels at a sport, most future Olympians will practice outside of school hours and join a more competitive team. From there, they can be discovered by a coach or representative from their national team.

When Olympians enter a new environment, like a national team, they can learn from people who are better than them. The most important part of being an athlete is staying dedicated to practicing. It's the only way we get better! With enough practice and a little bit of luck, athletes can be selected to become an Olympian and represent their country!

How do athletes represent their country? Do their names get picked from a big top hat?

Olympians are selected by their countries to represent them at the Olympics. In individual events, each country can send up to three people. In team events, it's up to each nation to select their team. The number of people on each team will depend on the sport. Each country has a different set of rules and requirements for selecting athletes to represent them in the Olympics.

Most countries will host a national championship or Olympic Trial to find the very best athletes in each event. In order to compete in the trial or championship, you have to be the best of the best! Team sports, like soccer, usually nominate players to join the national team, whereas in individual sports, such as running or swimming, athletes must first qualify with a set time in order to compete in a trial to earn a spot.

For athletes with dual-citizenship, meaning they are eligible to represent more than one country, they have to choose which country they would like to compete for and attend that country's national trials or participate on their national team.

For example, if a person immigrated to a country at a young age, they'd be able to represent the country they were born in or the country they're currently living in. Which one they choose to represent is entirely up to them!

The choice is yours!

FUN FACT
About 6% of athletes who participated in the 2018 Winter Games competed for a country they weren't born in!

How do you know what sport you can play in the Olympics? Are they randomly assigned?

You can compete in whatever Olympic sport you like! There are lots to choose from with more being added every two years! From team sports to individuals, winter to summer, there's a sport for every kind of person.

skateboarding

TOKYO 2020

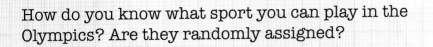

While anybody can technically participate in any sport, most Olympians choose their event based on their individual skills and their geographical location. For example, there are fewer cross-country skiers from Thailand than there are from Canada. It's hard to do a winter sport if you live in a warm place!

Another factor in picking your sport is the sporting culture where you live. What sports are popular where you grew up? Maybe your town loves soccer, maybe they love curling, maybe they love table tennis. You're more likely to participate in a sport that's popular in your area.

How do Olympians embody the Olympic spirit? Is the Olympic spirit a ghost that flies around the Olympic village?

Not that kind of spirit! The Olympics exists for many reasons, but above all, it exists to bring people together and lift others up. That's the Olympic spirit!

What makes Olympians so special isn't just that they're good at a sport. That's only part of it! What makes Olympians especially memorable are all the things they do that display exceptional character. Olympians are remembered for gold-medal performances, but more importantly, they are remembered for the people they are.

There have been many memorable Olympic moments over the years, but the ones that stick with us are the ones in which the athletes show their love for the sport, their opponents, and their community.

American 5,000m runner Abbey Cooper helped a fellow runner during a race. Canadian 800m runner Lindsey Butterworth helped feed those in need in her community. Japanese tennis player Naomi Osaka is outspoken about mental health support. American gymnast Simone Biles received the Presidential Medal of Freedom. These are just a few of the remarkable athletes who help us remember that the Olympics aren't only about sports.

LINDSEY BUTTERWORTH

ABBEY COOPER

FUN FACT

Abbey Cooper helped Nikki Hamblin of New Zealand up when they both fell over during qualifying. She encouraged Nikki to finish the race and although Abbey was injured, she also finished the race.

NAOMI OSAKA

SIMONE BILES

FUN FACT

Simone Biles is the youngest person to receive the Presidential Medal of Freedom. She received the award for excellence in gymnastics and for her work as an advocate for mental health and safety.

How do athletes win a gold medal? Do they perform their very best in their event, sometimes break records, and make their country proud?

YES! Athletes can earn a gold, silver, or bronze medal for placing 1st, 2nd, or 3rd in their events! Winning a medal and standing on the podium is a huge accomplishment for athletes who train tirelessly to become Olympians, but with or without a medal, Olympians leave each Summer and Winter Games with so much more!

FUN FACT

The host country designs the Olympic medals for that year!

1st

Gold

2nd

Silver

3rd

Bronze

1st

2nd

3rd

FUN FACT
The first place athlete's national anthem is played as they receive their medal! This tradition began at the 1932 Games.

FUN FACT
The Olympic Motto is "Citius, Altius, Fortius" which is Latin for "Faster, Higher, Stronger."

Follow your dreams!

The Olympics is about finding something you love doing and trying to become the best you can be. It's about being a good teammate and knowing that when we lift up the people around us, everyone wins. It's about being fair and giving all people an equal chance at doing their best. These are the qualities that make Olympians great, but they are also qualities that make any person great!

FUN FACT

April 6 is the International Day of Sport for Development and Peace. It is a day to encourage peace and understanding and recognize the impact sports have on social change and community development.

We watch the Olympics on TV, partly to see the sports, but mostly to watch other people do extraordinary things. Those extraordinary things are usually not about the actual sport but rather about watching them stay calm under pressure, put others before themselves, and work hard to make their dreams come true. While we all won't be Olympians, everyone who tries their best in their heart is an Olympian.

HOST YOUR VERY OWN OLYMPIC GAMES IN YOUR BACKYARD

You can capture the spirit of the Olympics at home! Invite your friends for a day full of events inspired by the Games.

MAKE YOUR OWN OLYMPIC TORCH

Grab a **flashlight**, some **tissue paper** (**red**, **yellow**, and **orange**), **aluminum foil**, and some **tape**. Wrap the aluminum foil around the handle of the flashlight. Then tape strips of tissue paper above the light to represent the flames. When you turn on the flashlight, your torch will glow!

REPRESENT YOUR FAVORITE COUNTRY

Have fun researching and learning about countries from around the world. Choose one you like and wear clothes in the colors of that country's flag to compete. Before you get started, host an opening ceremony where you and your friends all share a fun fact about the country you are representing!

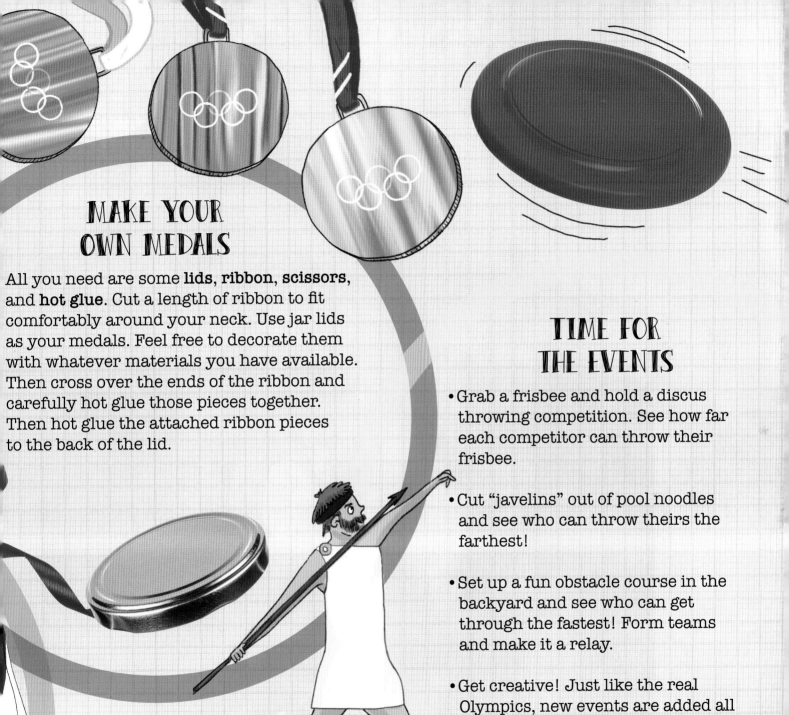

MAKE YOUR OWN MEDALS

All you need are some **lids**, **ribbon**, **scissors**, and **hot glue**. Cut a length of ribbon to fit comfortably around your neck. Use jar lids as your medals. Feel free to decorate them with whatever materials you have available. Then cross over the ends of the ribbon and carefully hot glue those pieces together. Then hot glue the attached ribbon pieces to the back of the lid.

TIME FOR THE EVENTS

• Grab a frisbee and hold a discus throwing competition. See how far each competitor can throw their frisbee.

• Cut "javelins" out of pool noodles and see who can throw theirs the farthest!

• Set up a fun obstacle course in the backyard and see who can get through the fastest! Form teams and make it a relay.

• Get creative! Just like the real Olympics, new events are added all the time. Try to create fun games of your own.

MEET OLYMPIAN MADELEINE KELLY

Meet Canadian national champion and Olympian Madeleine Kelly. Madeleine started running track around the age of 12. She was inspired by Melissa Bishop-Nriagu, a runner who made her Olympic debut at the London 2012 Games. Madeleine continued to run and train and eventually went to run track in college at the University of Toronto. She claimed her first Canadian 800m title in 2019 after taking home bronze at the famous Harry Jerome Track Classic. She earned a bronze medal at the Canadian Olympic Trials, giving her the chance to compete at the 2020 Tokyo Olympic Games. Madeleine is training for the upcoming Games and when she is not running, she writes for a magazine about running. She also wrote this book!